Element

Element

Kim Cope Tait

LEAPING DOG
P·R·E·S·S

Raleigh, North Carolina / 2017

The author and publisher would like to thank Bamboo Ridge for publishing "Resistance of a Poem."

Book and cover design by Jordan Jones.

ISBN 978-1-58775-016-8

Tait, Kim Cope.
Element.

Printed in the United States of America.

SECOND EDITION

Leaping Dog Press
Jordan Jones, Editor & Publisher
PO Box 90125
Raleigh, NC 27676-0125
www.leapingdogpress.com

Contents

Spring

Summer

Fall

Spring

Flame Sestina

She lets her crimson mantle slip
down the slick edge of her want,
enfold on itself at her ankles. Her tongue,
restless in the mouth, still quiet like a bird
poised on its brittle branch. Flame
of this pathos: a pale, steady light

in unfathomable darkness. She lights
a way for her own fear, turns and slips
into the hollow of her own flameless
soul. Cold. *It's not that I want*
this or that, I touch the bird
with my own life, know the pink tongue

inside the yellow beak. Tongue
like a slender blade of grass, light
in the tiny avian head, bird
promise, this night, this. Night. Slip
fingers under feathered body, lift want
from the hollow of its tender throat. Flame

ignites the vision of a long kiss goodbye. Flame
lifting this heat, curling around the tongue,
inhalation of fresh desire: a want
so abstract, so florid. Full. Light.
Phosphorescent need chirps as we slip
beneath the surface and the bird

tumbles from that branch, bird
of love, bird of heat, energy, flame
kindled by this thing we slip
under our bodies as we sleep. Tongues
wagging just beyond our thought, light
singing at the edge of citrus dreams, *I want*

this, too she whispers, *I want
too.* And she is the flesh-colored bird
crouching in the corner of our minds, light
moving across her like water, like flames,
listless combustion, moving like tongues
in air. We resist this, let slip

our own brilliant fear. *I want light
I am the bird. I am the thing that slips
to the floor, flame of the stillest tongue.*

On Riding the "Lemming Board"

for Joel

This boy. This
moment.
My sun rises
in this space
between being and
unbeing. Seconds
where my world
is striated: asphalt —
yellow grasses nodding,
rocking — pale ocean
lifting, falling — sky
big, heavy: painted
dome over our heads.
Your lanky body
against it. The way
you bend low, smooth
crescent of torso,
arms curved in a
hollow arc over you
in your moment of
liberation. In mine.
Shared thing unnameable.
Like need, like salt
air settling on skin.
Touch the diaphanous

net of our unwords.
Wheels and motion.
Light glints off of
passing cars. Something
held in my hand, something
perfect.
I would give it to you, this
thing. But I want so
to name it.

Impulse

A wildness that frightens. Appetite
for the unbound. The infinite. What I
might do — turn to the sun, turn to a too
bright light. Kiss someone hard on the lips:
full mouth of my wanting. Leap into the
fire that flickers against the white bone of my
rib cage.

This thing — held. Guarded. I linger
in this unsafe place. Lick its dangerousness.
Wipe my mouth with the back of my hand
and balance on the thin line I have
drawn for myself in white chalk.
Tiny motes lift off, one by one,
flakes of some division
still wanting to be.

They disintegrate into air, and I am
without boundary. Without borders in the country
of my self. It is a restlessness that threatens
dissolution. Immolation. I ignite. I lift off
and move untended into a trajectory so high
I slip into some foreign orbit. Float
lonely as a cloud, and even Blake
waves to me as I go by, himself
well within the earth's atmosphere.

I cling to star and star and star—celestial monkey
bars. I obstruct the sun's light with my own
blazing body. Afire, I am set afire.
I consider the irony of light casting shadow,
mine cast on the moon, writhing mass of
self and this unruly flame. I am the thing
behind the icon, lurking. The shapeless
infinity that fills the ears when we
sleep to dream.

Kim Cope Tait

Whisper

Voice emerges like a
dove passes between
the lips is breath is
a prism of every thought
that has passed
since that day.
It is my penance my
lament, the ways in which
I know myself as other
than what I want to be.
I am
vulgar, crude, untamed, mis-
shapen. I am the blue
of that background, dappled
with the shadows of unself of
wanting and wanting and
finally — Nothing. The emptiness
of a vast field. My hair as
long and bending shafts of
wheat and grass and
dandelions gone to
seed. I am the un-
mother the un-woman. Super,
Hyper, over, thing of
my blindness. I grope in
darkness, cold air of the un-
day. Un-love. Un-language.
Dis-being.

Insatiable

I.

Walking away from me, you are the boy
Isawbefore.Yourbodymoveseasily
between the flickering of this pale sun
and your long shadow, cast on the ground
in front of you. The sun has risen
from my navel, sits high in a stark
sky. I am left with my words,
like petals or leaves, scattered
around me. I will collect them.

They are all, I used to say.
They are all. I gather the words
with my hands, carry them in my skirts.
Count them and reorder them, fine
endowment of meaning ... but what
truth? What truth is contained here?
Truth of my high-pitched longing?

II.

There is no middle place. Either I
can't breathe, or I am over-oxygenated,
gills open too wide, choking on this
excessive air. I have no way to contain
what spills from my heart like water, like

love. And it is neither water nor love but
bitterness and bliss, strung together in one
equivocal braid that makes me whinny
this mounting laugh-cry like a horse
alone in a wide open space. Wide open
space. I am not the thing I thought I was
before. I am no thing. No thing.

III.

I begin
to dismantle the tower. The weight
of the stones in my hands is pleasing,
but the tower itself is all wrong. I am not meant
for this altitude. Not meant for these heights.
When the tower is gone, and I wash my words
from my body, I am purified by action. I am
a child again, new. A new thing, yes. But rebellious
child that I am, I will still lift myself on air, still
climb up through clouds, searching for that thing.
 I will be like Icarus who poor thing flew too close
to the sun. I will ignite, brilliant specter arcing
in this forbidden sky. I will be gone. I will be
gone.

Spill

It doesn't get fixed. I don't
know how not to want what I
can't have. How not to be
the thing I am: a dandelion
gone to seed. I bow my head
before the pale sun, let
each particle lift from my core, drift
on air ... away from stem, away
from soul. Shadow
moving inside of shadow, I
can't have touch...that thing
you don't seem to need. It is
this same that I crave. Can
taste it on my pink tongue ...
but to drink. O, to drink that thing.
Drink it till it's gone.
Until I am gone. No matter.
I am Tori, I am Tori. Leaving, lifting
off. Twisting, tangling
we are language, we are tree
trunks, clouds in a halo
around a mountain top. We are one
we are. Perfect ebullience
of what expands and contracts,
pulses. Turns and lightens.
Glides on a stream of consciousness.
Litmus thought. Air. Light. Vapor.
Phosphorescent bird inside the
flame

Kim Cope Tait

of a secret sestina. I grow cold.
I grow old. I grow into this aloneness
again. Solitary ... having passed through
your light, your exuberance. Your
near-love, near-care. To be the subject
of such passion, such raw and unpretentious
language. Yes. Please.

Summer

Sun Sestina

I close my hand over the boy's
hand. He can see that my sun
has set into my throat, knows
my wanting, feels it like an animal
in the dark underbelly of these days.
We breathe unwords, move across

water on our bellies, on our feet. Across
this distance I sing down the boy:
sing the belligerent truth of my silence. Day
of undoing, come. My language is a big sun,
yellow and bald in its laughter, the animal
radiance of this heat. In this moment I know

there is no place for this thing. I know
the impossibility, the imperfection that spans across
every single star, white pointy eyes of animals
that haunt the dream, lick their lips, sigh the boy,
sigh the name, hunt the motionless sun,
mother of them all. They will not find her today,

caught in my throat as she is. I swallow and day
becomes mine. Owner of illusion, ready to know
what can't be known. Poised on this brink: sun
burning a hole in my gut, burning, burning across
generations of lovers in their galaxies, orbit of this boy,
this light. I turn in the dark exterior, my animal

want rolling inside my rib cage like marbles, animal
hunger, animal need, infant truth burgeoning. Day
dawns in my pelvis, lifting itself down, and the boy
turns away, walks. How can he know
the meaning of a sun rising from my navel, moving across
the planet of my body, glistening the undoing of all the suns

ever arched in desire across this fatal sky. O sun
of being, sun of mine, lift me into that orbit. Animals,
move in my heart, make me weak, breathe across
the taut strings of my self, create a music so fair that days
will move inside of it. I move in this unknown
rhythm. Become soil. Root. Leaf of what the boy

raises like a banner above his head, across sunlight
so fervent in its heat, boy in the animal dream, the
day peaking in his man-heart. Know this: love.

Kim Cope Tait

Me and Mrs. Dalloway

What I am, I say equivocally and step into the waves.
It is a whisper, and like everything else, it only
has meaning for me. There is still comfort in this.
And terror. Memory flickers across a pale horizon:
touching my sons. Their apples for cheeks in my
hands. Their clipped hair as my fingers move
against its angle, gently now. Mommy.

I feel so strange. Foreigner in my own edemic body.
I float. Far out at sea. Me and Clarissa. Bobbing
at the surface. *To live even one day is so dangerous,*
she reminds me, and I recognize it as the song that
lives me; it fills the air above our heads. Dangerous.
Dangerous. It is a resounding threat. Echo of a
promise. A yes. This undoing. Me. We come undone.
We two out on the sea, we unravel, disclose what we are
to a hostile jury of gulls, poised mid-flight and hovering
over what they do not know and cannot guess.

I am a shambles, I observe, but this is nothing new.
I take Clarissa in my thin arms, but she kisses me
on my pink lips and begins to sink. I let her
fawn-colored hair slip softly through my fingers
as she descends in shafts of indecisive light. She
leaves me: modern-day Ophelia. She. Good bye,
Clarissa. What can I be but this thing that remains?
What can I be but this?

Resistance of a Poem

Full expression of the lotus blooming in my pelvis: bony
white structure that contains this quiet exuberance —

       the poem tumbles apart.
              Cascades off into distant air.
Mist over rocks at Waipio: what the waterfall gives to the sky.

       The way we receive it
              there among the waves, lifting and
crumbling around us, inside of us. There is no explanation

       for this. The way I — no,
             there are no words, I say, but secretly
I know that there are only words. That language is all and that

the dangerous syllables of my wildness will undo me. It is a
curse, it is a promise. Unraveling the self: it aches, it saves.

Unbearable

And so these words pass between us on barely tempered air. I
laugh and turn my head in the way that means I am playing,

keeping up, but the way my heart breaks to think of you
wanting to shape me, bend me to your will, is something

of which I will not speak. Is this what you do with care?
This is too much hurt for me to bear, and yet I cannot cut you loose.

You are that light, that vision divine, what I hold to my hollow
chest and believe will save me from all of the decisions I did not

make. You are the boy in the animal dream, and even as I say it,
I know that it is too much for you to carry.

It is too much for me to ask of you--to be the bearer of this
unbearable want. I think it hurts you too,

and when I say I can't resist you, I mean it in so many ways
it makes me turn my face in shame.

Real

Burgeoning, billowing, lifting
on air — such intensity, such
light. You are the thing
that rises above them all, hovers
for a moment, and is gone.
Gentle phosphorescence
of such clarity.

Time clings to your back like
shadow, like memory, like
every impossibility ever
revealed to you, like what
it takes to let something go.
Really let it go. You. If only
you could see it now. What
wild freedom awaits you —
a single breath away. Go.

Be the thing that you are. Live and
love. You of the animal dream, you
of the living language. Do not be afraid
to be alive. It is a delicious thing
to know oneself as you do. It is
what everyone holds their mirrors up to,
trying to catch a reflection, trying to
absorb something they cannot name,
cannot be. Show us how to wield that
 light. Show us the truth of your existence,

so perfectly entwined with earth and sky
and sea.

You make things with your hands. Shape
souls out of living materials, give voice
to the trunks of trees. Intrepid artist, builder,
rider of waves, tamer of butterflies. Sleep,
friend, in the palm of this heart, in the knowing:
there is more love in the world than you can fathom
and loving someone so much that it feels like hurt
is the kind of thing that makes us real.

Fall

Snow Sestina

I rest in the stark and leaning limbs
of this crooked tree, study the arch
of branch against light-fretted sky. Cold
shadow of this tangle falls lightly on snow,
moves against air — pulse of my invisible
want. Perched here I am hungry

for what aches, what saves. Hunger
for something I will not name but lift my limbs
to praise, beckon. That ruinous light: you. Invisible
guest in my unholy sanctuary, arched
against this delicate web of branches, snow
still in your mussed hair. Melting now. But cold.

The words pass between us: *I grow cold,*
I say. *I grow old,* like a promise from hungry
lips. *I die again,* I say, and lick the snow
from your forehead, wrap my tender limbs
around you in the fullest arch
of my ravenous embrace. *We are invisible*

I tell myself, but we are not. Vision
divine: crumbles in my hands. See the cold
hand that parts us. See the arch
of spine, twist of bodies pushing against hunger
so great it bends branches, snaps limbs
that stretch across sky. Quiet thud in pale snow.

Silhouette of us, falling into softest snow,
gently tangled, perfectly entwined. Invisible
circuit of energy through our thin limbs,
this latticed structure of selves. *I grow cold.*
I grow old. I turn to stone. I know my hunger
as the thing that will undo me. Arch

the soul, resist the want, the fall, the arch
of sky fretted with some foreign discord. Snow
is the quietest way an element can be. This hunger
spills itself across glistening white: vision
of this imperfect thing dissipating, sinking into cold
memory. I let it go I — let it go. My limbs

turn to ice. I am undone, I say, my hunger arched
on the snow before us, outlined by the shadow limbs
of this crumbling tree. Cold vision of what cannot be.

Kim Cope Tait

The Kiss

Your mouth is an "o."
Pale pink lips and the circle
of your word, your breath,
your surprise as I kiss you,
graze your white teeth
with my intrepid tongue.

It's the only way to say
good bye, I whisper …
with the body. I dreamt
this kiss for months, ran
my fingers over your ribs,
caressing them one by one.
Kisses for each.

"O," you say,
and it is the perfect sound
of the distance already
spun out into this valley
of future — echo of longing
and contentment
at once. *Good bye*, I say,
and they are the last
syllables of us.

What We Are

for Andrea

Snow hangs in your hair
and you stand on the threshold.
I know you in this body, this cosmic
wave of light. We are wide awake
and we are this perfect thing that
cannot be named. Women, yes.
Sisters — mmm. One. We are
one and I hop into an image of you,
walk around there, feel the cool
moss beneath my feet. Matching
pictures, you say. Identically.

I whisper and my breath spans
the galaxy: warm air of this exultation,
this knowing. What you offer is
forgiveness, a gentle refusal to censure me
in your wisdom, but instead to pull me
to your breast, say *Here — listen.*
And I listen to that quiet rhythm:
your heart given to what you have
chosen. I learn its pattern, learn
the soft beat of sacrifice and the
truth about too much or too little fire.

I learn you, and I learn myself. I see
the way to balance on the edge of this

vast space and not fall. Not
fall. Yes and yes and this moment
like the pale sky of an Alaska night —
you are suspended there. Still visible.
Glittering Northern star. You know
what it is to want. Don't crumble,
I say, don't slip down the pink veil of
sky into the sea. Your words heal, they

guide, even as they scatter, picked up
by the wind of your own desire, tossed
into air on such uncertainty. Truth
bandied about on what makes us
strangers to the rest of the world, to our
men. Let us go now and be
the things that we are.

Last Words

Septimus cries for the way we hurt each other.
It is hard to believe that Virginia Woolf wrote me
so many years before my birth. Wrote you.

We are not crazy, you said, just misunderstood,
and I smiled at the cliché of the thing and at
the way you said we, because I loved you then,

and knew that in your reassurance you meant
to show me finally, that you felt as connected to me
as I did to you. I loved you even more for that.

Wept as you drove away, tinted windows hiding
you while I stood in the naked sunlight, filtering
down through the moving branches of a mango tree.

Tara Sestina

She lifts herself out, sees the way to rise
from the full ruin of her own creation,
sees the ashes sift through the heavy air
and come to rest on her forehead—quiet
aftermath of her own desire exploding
against a perfect sky: *This is real,*

he says, turning the goddess in his hand. Real.
Bronze image of Tara, said to have risen
from the tears of the boddhisattva. Creation
of feminine compassion from man's suffering.
To help him in his work, she says, quiet
ache in her own throat, letting breath

leave her body without sound, silent sigh
of surrender. She wants to say this: *Real,*
like the way I love, like the inquietude
of my smoldering self, like learning to rise
from the wreckage that my own hand creates
even now as I give you this: explosion

of hope. This is what finally explodes:
the convergence of truth and fiction in air,
the two colliding, sudden creation
of fragments — arcing jetsam of a real
but unrecoverable thing. What rises
on that grey wave and collapses quietly.

And even as it does collapse, she is quiet.
Offers herself up in the silent explosion
that her own offering begets. She rises
because it is desire — not self — cast into air,
because what remains is real:
her compassion and his longing. Creation

from destruction. Her love created
from his bitterness. The absence of words
to accompany a parting gift — real
expression of her gratitude. Dreams explode
at an alarming rate, but she catches sparks mid-air
and knows about her wholeness. She rises,

finds her place. Goddess of nothing she can name, real creator
of her own risen destiny, she learns to give thanks to the quiet
boddhisattva, whose longing exploded in her own heart.

Leaping Dog Press, *featuring* Asylum Arts Press

Applebaum, Samuel. ***Chtcheglov: Poems.*** Asylum Arts.

Applebaum, Samuel. ***Judea Capta: A Long Poem.*** Asylum Arts.

Aufderheide, Charles. ***Garden of Games: The Collected Poems of Charles E. Aufderheide.*** Asylum Arts.

Basso, Eric. ***Accidental Monsters: Poems & Texts, 1976.*** Asylum Arts.

Basso, Eric. ***Bartholomew Fair: Fiction.*** Asylum Arts.

Basso, Eric. ***The Beak Doctor: Short Fiction, 1972–1976.*** Asylum Arts.

Basso, Eric. ***Catafalques: Poems, 1987–1989.*** Asylum Arts.

Basso, Eric. ***The Catwalk Watch: Poems, 1977–1979.*** Asylum Arts.

Basso, Eric. ***Enigmas: Short Plays, 1979–1982.*** Asylum Arts.

Basso, Eric. ***Ghost Light: Poems, 1990–1994.*** Asylum Arts.

Basso, Eric. ***The Golem Triptych: A Dramatic Trilogy.*** Asylum Arts.

Basso, Eric. ***The Sabattier Effect: with incidental music composed & arranged by the author.*** Asylum Arts.

Basso, Eric. ***The Smoking Mirror: Poems, 1980–1986.*** Asylum Arts.

Baudelaire, Charles. (Kendall Lappin, translator) ***Echoes of Baudelaire: Selected Poems.*** Asylum Arts.

Bernard, Kenneth. ***The Baboon in the Nightclub: A Poem.*** Asylum Arts.

Bernard, Kenneth. ***How We Danced While We Burned, followed by La Justice, or The Cock That Crew: Two Plays.*** Asylum Arts.

Bernard, Kenneth. ***The Qui Parle Play & Poems.*** Asylum Arts.

Boyd, Greg. ***Carnival Aptitude: Being an Exuberance in Short Prose and Photomontage.*** Asylum Arts.

Boyd, Greg. ***The Double: Doppelangelgänger: An Annotated Novel.*** LDP Book #4.

Boyd, Greg. ***The Nambuli Papers: A Multimedia Novel.*** LDP Book #6.

Boyd, Greg. ***Water & Power: Stories.*** Asylum Arts.

Cull, Mark E. ***One Way Donkey Ride: Short Fiction.*** Asylum Arts.

Daumal, René. (Jordan Jones, translator) ***Mugle: A Novella.*** LDP Book #8. Forthcoming in 2005.

Dixon, Stephen. ***Friends: More Will and Magna Stories.*** Asylum Arts.

Ducornet, Rikki. ***Two Essays.*** LDP Chapbook #3. Forthcoming.

Fondation, Larry. ***Common Criminals: L.A. Crime Stories.*** Asylum Arts.

Gordon, Kirpal. *What We Got against Tyranny: Prose Poems.* LDP Chapbook #1.

Hendershot, Cynthia. *City of Mazes and Other Tales of Obsession.* Asylum Arts.

Hood, Charles. *The Xopilote Cantos.* Asylum Arts.

Jones, Jordan. *The Wheel: Poems.* LDP Book #11.

Kostelanetz, Richard. *Minimal Fictions.* Asylum Arts.

Lappin, Kendall (translator) *Dead French Poets Speak Plain English: An Anthology of Poetry.* Asylum Arts.

Lappin, Kendall. *Memoirs of a Translator of Poetry.* Asylum Arts.

Lappin, Kendall (translator). *The Muse Spoke French: An Anthology of Poetry.* Asylum Arts.

Martin, Joe. *Parabola: Shorter Fictions.* Asylum Arts.

Martin, Richard. *Marks: Poems.* Asylum Arts.

Martin, Richard. *Modulations: Poems.* Asylum Arts.

Martin, Stephen-Paul. *The Gothic Twilight: Short Fiction.* Asylum Arts.

Martin, Stephen-Paul. *Instead of Confusion: Fiction.* Asylum Arts.

Nerval, Gérard de. (Kendall Lappin, translator) *Aurélia followed by Sylvie: Fiction.* Asylum Arts.

Papadimitrakopoulos, Elias. *Toothpaste with Chlorophyll & Maritime Hot Baths: Stories.* Asylum Arts.

Peters, Robert. *Mad Ludwig of Bavaria & Other Short Plays: Drama.* Asylum Arts.

Peters, Robert. *Poems: Selected & New 1967–1991.* Asylum Arts.

Peters, Robert. *Where the Bee Sucks: Workers, Drones and Queens of Contemporary American Poetry.* Asylum Arts.

Redonnet, Marie. (Gilbert Alter-Gilbert, translator) *Dead Man & Company: Poems.* LDP Book #7.

Redonnet, Marie. (Jordan Stump, translator) *Understudies: Stories.* LDP Book #9.

Richman, Elliot. *Franz Kafka's Daughter Meets the Evil Nazi Empire!!!: The Heroism of Roaches: Holocaust-tainted Poems.* Asylum Arts.

Richman, Elliot. *Honorable Manhood: Poems of Eros & Dust.* Asylum Arts.

Richman, Elliot. *The World Dancer: Poems.* Asylum Arts.

Roditi, Edouard. *Choose Your Own World.* Asylum Arts.

Romero, Norberto Luis. (H. E. Francis, translator) *Last Night of Carnival & Other Stories.* LDP Book #5.

Shaffer, Eric Paul. *Lāhaina Noon: Nā Mele O Maui: Poems.* LDP Book #10.

Shaffer, Eric Paul. *Living at the Monastery, Working in the Kitchen: Poems.* LDP Book #3.

Shaffer, Eric Paul. *Portable Planet: Poems.* LDP Book #1.

Stoloff, Carolyn. *You Came to Meet Someone Else: Poems.* Asylum Arts.

Tait, Kim Cope. *Element: Poems.* LDP Chapbook #2.

Wisniewski, Mark. *All Weekend with the Lights On: Stories.* LDP Book #2.

Leaping Dog Press / Asylum Arts books are available in fine bookstores everywhere, on the Internet at leapingdogpress.com and Amazon.com, or by contacting:

Leaping Dog Press
PO Box 90125
Raleigh, NC 27676-0125

When ordering direct, include $3 for the first book, and $1.50 for each additional book for shipping. North Carolina residents should add sales tax.

Photo: Cayson Peterson

About the Author

Kim Cope Tait earned her MFA in Writing at Vermont College of Fine Arts in 2000. Her work has appeared in literary journals and magazines in the U.S. and abroad. Kim also wrote and recorded *Lotus Wheel: Guided Meditations for Relaxation and Healing* in 2013. Having lived in California, Hawaii, Switzerland, New Zealand, and Vermont, Kim now lives with her family and teaches in the High Rockies of Colorado.

www.ingramcontent.com/pod-product-compliance
Lightning Source LLC
Chambersburg PA
CBHW071438040426
42445CB00012BA/1387